D1711845

From the Factory

Contents

Nancy White

What Do Factories Make?

Where have you seen these things?
Where were they made?

All these things were made in **factories**.

What else do you think is made in a factory?

What Is a Factory?

A factory is a building where things are made. You make things at home, too, but your home is not a factory. Why not?

How is a factory different from a home?	
Home	**Factory**
Things are made one at a time.	Things are made in large numbers.
Things are made to be used at home.	Things are made to be sold in stores.
Homes are usually small.	Factories are often very big.

We say things made in a factory are **manufactured**.

Factories use different materials to make finished products.

Some factories make potato chips. Potatoes are the **raw material** for potato chips.

The potatoes are washed, peeled, sliced, and cooked. Then the potato chips are put in bags and shipped to stores.

Cotton cloth is made in a factory. Cotton from cotton plants is the raw material.

The cotton is spun into thread and then woven into cloth. The cloth may be made into clothing at another factory.

How Does a Factory Work?

In a bicycle factory, one person works on the bicycle frame, another person makes the wheels, and someone else paints the bikes.

In a factory that makes washing machines, different people work on different parts of the machine.

In most factories, each person works on just one part of a thing.

In many factories, people work on an **assembly line**.

At a car factory, the cars move along an assembly line. Each worker puts together or works on a different part of the car.

t the end, a finished car rolls off the ssembly line.

Machines and People at Work

Many of the jobs in a factory are done by machines.

There are machines that mix things.

There are machines that fill **containers**.

ook at what this machine does!

Machines do many jobs in a factory, but machines need people to work them.

This person is **inspecting** thread. Could a machine do this job?

ome jobs are done by **robots**. This robot is
ust an arm. It doesn't have a head or a body.

 robot is run by a computer. But a person
as to **program** the computer, or "teach" it
hat to do.

Made in a Factory

Toothbrushes and baseball gloves, potato chips and ice cream, cars, washing machines and even toys—many things we see and use every day are made in factories.

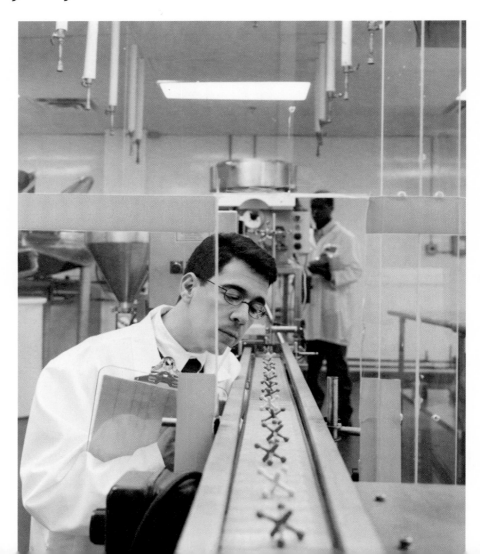